STUDY GUIDE

Marks of a Healthy Church

Mark Dever & Jonathan Leeman

LIGONIER.ORG | 800-435-4343

Copyright © 2016 Ligonier Ministries
421 Ligonier Court, Sanford, FL 32771
E-mail: info@ligonier.org
All rights reserved.
No reproduction of this work without permission.
Printed in the United States of America.

1

What Is the Church?

INTRODUCTION

To understand what the church is, we must first have an idea about what the church is supposed to be. In this lesson, Dr. Dever examines Paul's first letter to the Corinthians to show us how the church is to reflect God's character.

LESSON OBJECTIVES

1. To define the church as reflected in God's holiness, unity, and love
2. To emphasize the church's great responsibility in reflecting God's holiness, unity, and love

SCRIPTURE READING

For just as the body is one and has many members, and all the members of the body, though many, are one body, so it is with Christ.

—1 Corinthians 12:12

LECTURE OUTLINE

A. The church is to be holy.
   1. Holiness is strangeness to the world and a special relationship with God.
      a. The church consists of those called to be holy and blameless, those set apart from the world in a special relationship with God.
      b. Our message and wisdom is different than the message and wisdom of the world, which is one of the central themes of 1 Corinthians 1–2.

  c. Christians are God's temple, and because God's temple is sacred, the church is called to be pure (1 Cor. 3:16).
 2. God has always been concerned with the purity of His people.
  a. In 1 Corinthians 5, Paul addressed the sexual sin of the church.
  b. Paul appeals to the Corinthians with the same refrain that God spoke to the Israelites who were preparing to enter the Promised Land (1 Cor. 5:13).
 3. Holiness is an essential part of the Christian life.
  a. Paul argues that Christians have been washed and sanctified, and they will be resurrected. As a result, what Christians do with their bodies is significant (1 Cor. 6).
  b. Paul argues that the resurrection underscores God's concern for what is done with the body in this life.
  c. Paul pleads with the Corinthians to remember Israel and not to fall into idolatrous, evil desires (1 Cor. 10:1–13).
 4. Holiness is to be an attribute that marks the church.
  a. Holiness is our constant striving after a God-honoring way of life.
  b. Holiness is an essential part of the church, and that is why so many aspects of the church reinforce our need to be holy.

B. The church is to be united.
 1. Christians are supposed to be separated from the world, not from each other, because unity is a distinguishing mark of the church (1 Cor. 3:1–4).
 2. Unity gives testimony to the truth of the gospel.
  a. Unity transcended the division between Jew and Gentile, and every worldly division is to be transcended by the unity found in Christ.
  b. Paul is especially distraught to see division during the Lord's Supper, a feast of unity (1 Cor. 11:17–34).

C. The church is to be loving.
 1. First Corinthians 8–14 is a long excursus on the topic of love, dealing with showing consideration toward others, because love is how Christians are unified.
 2. Love builds up the church (1 Cor. 8:1).
  a. Paul's principle of love: "Let no one seek his own good, but the good of his neighbor" (1 Cor. 10:24).
  b. Paul speaks of love as the most excellent way because it edifies the church.
 3. Love determines how the church is to function.
  a. Paul prioritizes prophecy over tongues, because prophecy edifies the church, and the most loving way to exercise gifts in the church is for the edification of others.
  b. Paul's practical application of love in 1 Corinthians 14 makes it as definitive of a chapter on love as 1 Corinthians 13.

4. Paul loved the church.
   a. Paul truly experienced the grace of God, calling himself "the least of the apostles" (1 Cor. 15:9) because he had persecuted the church.
   b. It is only fitting that it is Paul who urges the Corinthians to love one another and to do all things for the edification of the church.

D. Why should the church be holy, united, and loving?
   1. The church must be holy because God is holy.
      a. Paul exhorts, "Be imitators of me, as I am of Christ" (1 Cor. 11:1).
      b. Imitating Christ makes us different from the world; in Christ, God has set us apart (1 Cor. 1:2).
      c. The wisdom of God is not the wisdom of the world, and God's wisdom is the gospel, which is foolishness to the world (1 Cor. 2:12, 3:19).
      d. We are strange to the world because the world is estranged from God, so if we are going to belong to God, we will be like God.
      e. God has bought us and indwelt us, so we must be holy to reflect His holiness (1 Cor. 6:19–20).
   2. The church must be united because God is One.
      a. Paul reminded the Corinthians that the work of the church is all the work of God (1 Cor. 3:4–9).
      b. The one foundation of the church is Jesus Christ.
      c. Disunity tells a lie about God.
   3. The church must be loving because God is loving.
      a. Love for God must be at the center of our hearts as a response to His tremendous love for us.
      b. God took the initiative to redeem the church, so the church must reflect God's love to a dying world.

E. What is the church?
   1. The church is a congregation associated by covenant to the faith and fellowship of the gospel that observes the ordinances of Christ.
   2. The church is governed by Christ's laws—exercising the gifts, rights, and privileges in them, as expressed in His Word—in which there are two offices: elder and deacon.
   3. The church is the means by which we are called to display God's glorious character to His creation, by living for Him with a life of holiness, unity, and love.

STUDY QUESTIONS

1. The resurrection of the body has significant implications for our holiness and the holiness of the church.
   a. True
   b. False

2. A church's _____ most reflects God's redeeming grace to the world.
    a. Holiness
    b. Unity
    c. Love
    d. All of the above

3. Paul demonstrates how God has always desired His people to be holy by citing _____ when addressing the sexual immorality in Corinth.
    a. Genesis
    b. Deuteronomy
    c. Ecclesiastes
    d. Proverbs

4. Paul placed tongues over prophecy as the most loving expression of spiritual gifts at Corinth.
    a. True
    b. False

5. Paul argues for unity using the analogy of the _____.
    a. Body
    b. Spirit
    c. Cross
    d. Temple

6. Paul argues for holiness using the analogy of the _____.
    a. Body
    b. Spirit
    c. Cross
    d. Temple

DISCUSSION QUESTIONS

1. What are the different ways Paul argues that the church must be holy? Which do you find most compelling?

2. How does Paul's discussion of spiritual gifts relate to love?

3. What is the greatest problem caused by church disunity?

4. In what ways can you strive toward holiness, unity, and love in your local church?

2

Expositional Preaching

INTRODUCTION

Whether you are currently a member of a local church or are looking for a local church, knowing the marks of a healthy church is vital. In this lesson, Dr. Dever covers the first and most important mark of a healthy church: expositional preaching.

LESSON OBJECTIVES

1. To define expositional preaching
2. To emphasize the necessity of expositional preaching for church health

SCRIPTURE READING

Preach the word; be ready in season and out of season; reprove, rebuke, and exhort, with complete patience and teaching.

—2 Timothy 4:2

LECTURE OUTLINE

A. The first mark of a healthy church is expositional preaching.
   1. Expositional preaching is the ground on which all other marks of a healthy church take root and flourish by giving the Word of God priority.
   2. Expositional preaching is the basic diet of a local church.
      a. Expositional preaching is also known as expository preaching.
      b. Expositional preaching is often spoken of in contrast with topical preaching, though topical preaching isn't necessarily unbiblical.

B. What is expositional preaching?
   1. Scripture shapes expositional preaching.
      a. The heart of an expositional sermon comes directly from the heart of a particular passage of Scripture, seeking to unfold and explain it.
      b. We find an example of expositional preaching in the explaining of the law to the people of God in the book of Ezra.
   2. Expositional preaching is in service to the Word.
      a. Expositional preaching presumes the authority of God's Word.
      b. Preachers are called to bring God's Word to God's people and have authority only insofar as they preach God's Word.

C. Expositional preaching centers on the Word.
   1. God speaks through expositional preaching.
      a. Apart from God's revealing Himself in His Word, a preacher and a congregation will never get beyond what they already know.
      b. A preacher may teach a congregation about an important topic but never preach the point of a given passage of Scripture.
      c. A preacher committed to expositional preaching will preach a passage of Scripture in context to allow God's Word to speak.
      d. A preacher who doesn't preach expositionally runs the risk of only bringing a congregation up to his level.
   2. Preaching should be Word centered and Word directed, because God's Word creates and sustains God's people.
      a. God spoke and created all things (Gen. 1).
      b. God spoke and Abraham responded by faith (Gen. 12).
      c. God spoke and His people received the law (Ex. 20).
      d. God spoke and Ezekiel envisioned the life-giving Spirit (Ezek. 37).
   3. The Word is the central creative agent in all of Scripture and must be central in preaching because God saves by it alone.
      a. God made the world by His Word, came into the world by His Word, and saves the world by His Word (John 1; Rom. 10).
      b. When God's Word is heard, the Holy Spirit creates God's people.
   4. The Word is at the heart of Reformation theology.

D. Expositional preaching makes and matures Christians.
   1. God's Word is as essential to our growth as it was to our conversion.
      a. God feeds us through the Word (Duet. 8:3; Matt. 4:4).
      b. God cleanses us through the Word (Eph. 5:25–26).
   2. God's Word directs our lives and continually conforms us to Christ's image.
   3. God's Word is to be the substance of preaching.
      a. Preachers nurture God's people by preaching God's Word.
      b. The Holy Spirit does not use mere moral exhortations, history lessons, or social commentaries; the Holy Spirit uses God's Word.

4. God's Word is of the utmost priority.
    a. Paul told Timothy, "Preach the word" (2 Tim. 4:2), understanding it to be the "word of life" (Phil. 2:16).
    b. The office of deacon was created so that the Apostles could devote themselves "to prayer and the ministry of the word" (Acts 6:4).
5. God's Word is authoritative.
    a. Jesus and the Apostles quoted the Old Testament as the authoritative guide to the will and ways of God.
    b. Expositional preaching rests in the authority of God's Word.

E. Expositional preaching is what our culture needs.
    1. Expositional preaching is often wrongly considered outdated.
        a. People suggest that the church needs a less authoritarian, more artistic, and more communal approach to communicating God's truth.
        b. Expositional preaching may be the perfect medium to address a talkative, self-centered, confused, and anti-authoritarian culture.
    2. Expositional preaching does not need to be reshaped.
        a. We received God's grace through the Word; we did not contribute to our salvation.
        b. The idea that we must contribute something to make the Word more palatable is inconsistent.

F. Expositional preaching is not forever.
    1. A day will come when faith will give way to sight.
        a. We will one day see God (Rev. 22:4).
        b. Sermons are unique to this side of heaven.
        c. God's Word must be preached until that day.

G. Expositional preaching is a mark of a healthy church.
    1. The Word must be absolutely central, so that preaching has a particular content and transparency of form.
    2. The Word must be expected, such that church members should encourage, pray for, seek out, and thank God for Word-centered preaching.
    3. The Word is the truth, so preaching must convey that the Word is the only place in which truth can be found.

STUDY QUESTIONS

1. Many of the marks of a healthy church hinge on expositional preaching.
    a. True
    b. False

2. Expositional preaching is often contrasted with _____ preaching.
    a. Explanatory

b. Illustrative
c. Textual
d. Topical

3. The heart of expository preaching is _____.
   a. Scripture
   b. Illustration
   c. Application
   d. All of the above

4. The Holy Spirit does not use means to grow God's people.
   a. True
   b. False

5. _____ was used as a biblical example of expository preaching.
   a. Job
   b. Ezra
   c. Jonah
   d. Moses

6. The priority of the Word in the New Testament can be seen by the installment of _____.
   a. Apostles
   b. Prophets
   c. Deacons
   d. Elders

DISCUSSION QUESTIONS

1. What is the primary characteristic of expositional preaching? How is it related to God's creative power?

2. Why is expositional preaching important? What impact has expositional preaching had in your life?

3. What can a church wrongly prioritize over the Word? What detriment would such a wrong prioritization have to a congregation?

4. Why is expositional preaching the best method to reach our culture?

3

Biblical Theology

INTRODUCTION

Biblical theology teaches us to read the Bible as one story about the person and work of Christ. In this lesson, Dr. Leeman shows how biblical theology is not only central to how we are to read the Bible but also central to a healthy church.

LESSON OBJECTIVES

1. To define biblical theology as a hermeneutical method
2. To demonstrate how it contributes to the health of a church

SCRIPTURE READING

And beginning with Moses and all the Prophets, he interpreted to them in all the Scriptures the things concerning himself.

—Luke 24:27

Inquiring what person or time the Spirit of Christ in them was indicating when he predicted the sufferings of Christ and the subsequent glories.

—1 Peter 1:11

LECTURE OUTLINE

A. Biblical theology emphasizes the Bible as a whole.
   1. The story of Samson can be used as an example for considering a definition of biblical theology.

a. Samson was a mighty man, tearing apart a lion with his bare hands, and slaying a thousand Philistines with the jawbone of a donkey.
   b. Samson eventually told Delilah the secret of his strength and was taken prisoner, but he killed more Philistines in his death than in his life.
  2. The story of Samson should be understood and situated in biblical theology.
     a. Someone may teach about Samson's life in various ways that do not lend themselves to the broader scope of Scripture.
     b. Understanding what kind of book the Bible is will help us to see how it is all connected to Christ and has power to save (1 Peter 1:23).
  3. Biblical theology interprets the Bible within the entire storyline of the Bible.
     a. The storyline of the Bible culminates in the person and work of Christ.
     b. Biblical theology can be understood as a hermeneutical method of understanding Scripture as a single story.
  4. Biblical theology changes how we read the Bible.
     a. The Bible is not merely a religious encyclopedia or an instruction manual designed to give us inspiration and guidance.
     b. Biblical theology affirms that the Bible contains sixty-six books written over thousands of years by multiple authors in multiple genres; thus, the Bible can be read in many helpful ways.
     c. Biblical theology also affirms that God is the author of the entire Bible, superintending all of its human authors. This informs how we are to read the Bible.
     d. We can only understand parts of the Bible inasmuch as we understand how they contribute to the story of the Bible.

B. Biblical theology is a hermeneutical method rooted in Scripture.
  1. On the road to Emmaus, Jesus taught two disciples how to read the Bible.
     a. Jesus "opened their minds to understand the Scriptures" (Luke 24:45), showing them how everything written about Him in "the Law of Moses and the Prophets and the Psalms must be fulfilled" (Luke 24:44).
     b. The entire Old Testament spoke of Christ's suffering, resurrection, and the ensuing proclamation of repentance and forgiveness to the nations.
  2. Jesus rebuked the Pharisees for failing to see how the Bible is all about Him (John 5:39).
  3. The Apostles understood the Bible as one story about Jesus Christ (1 Cor. 15:3).
  4. The book of Hebrews testifies that the Bible is one story about Jesus.
     a. Nearly every chapter of the book of Hebrews shows how the Old Testament points to Jesus.
     b. The law, angels, Moses, the Promised Land, the Sabbath, the high priest, Melchizedek, the tabernacle, the sacrifices, and all the faithful point to Jesus.

C. Biblical theology connects stories like Samson's to the greater story of Jesus Christ.
   1. Samson is a type of Christ, meaning he prefigured some aspect of the person or work of Christ.
      a. Samson was a God-anointed judge empowered by the Holy Spirit.
      b. Samson was betrayed and handed over to enemies of God's people and yet rescued God's people by giving his life to those very enemies.
      c. Samson's life is meant to provoke our wonder for Christ who died for us in perfect humility and will return to judge the living and the dead.
   2. Biblical theology is powerful to save.
      a. Biblical theology shapes preaching in such a way that regardless of a passage's location, the entire plotline is in view.
      b. Preaching that is centered on the gospel—the person and work of Christ—is powerful to save (1 Peter 1:23).

D. Biblical theology is a mark of a healthy church.
   1. Biblical theology centers churches on the power of the gospel.
      a. The gospel is not moralism or mere motivation.
      b. The gospel is that which gives a sermon power.
   2. Biblical theology protects churches from error.
      a. Biblical theology keeps the Bible in context.
         i. For example, a prosperity preacher may take the covenant blessings and curses of Deuteronomy 28 out of context.
         ii. The relationship between blessing and obedience is clear, but Israel will soon suffer covenant curses.
         iii. Israel's disobedience points to our disobedience and the good news of a Savior in Jesus Christ.
      b. Biblical theology does not lose sight of the broad storyline of the Bible.
   3. Biblical theology shapes the church's mission because teaching that the Bible is all about the person and work of Christ shapes what a church will do.
   4. Biblical theology leads to worship.
      a. Understanding that everything in the Bible points towards Christ accompanies an overwhelming sense of God's love for us.
      b. The Bible—in fact, all of history—is purposed for the revelation of Jesus Christ. Being united to Him, we cannot help but worship.

STUDY QUESTIONS

1. Over the course of the lecture, Dr. Leeman defined biblical theology as theology that is faithful to what the Bible says.
   a. True
   b. False

2. Biblical theology can be understood as a _____ method of approaching the Bible.
   a. Literal
   b. Analogical
   c. Allegorical
   d. Hermeneutical

3. Jesus validates reading the Bible through the lens of biblical theology by teaching that the _____ spoke about Him.
   a. Law of Moses
   b. Prophets
   c. Psalms
   d. All of the above

4. People such as Samson, who function as a type of Christ, are rare in the Bible.
   a. True
   b. False

5. Biblical theology protects churches from error.
   a. True
   b. False

6. Biblical theology is important for _____.
   a. Doctrine
   b. Worship
   c. Missions
   d. All of the above

DISCUSSION QUESTIONS

1. What are the different ways that people approach the Bible? How do these approaches influence interpretation?

2. How is biblical theology a characteristic of the book of Hebrews? What are some examples?

3. Considering the purpose of biblical theology, what should we ask ourselves when studying various passages in our Bibles?

4. How does biblical theology contribute to the health of a church?

4

The Gospel

INTRODUCTION

The gospel is at the center of Scripture, the center of our faith, and the center of any healthy church. In this lesson, Dr. Leeman teaches how gospel-centeredness is the remedy to the internal challenges that confront churches.

LESSON OBJECTIVES

1. To define the gospel and the false gospels that threaten church health
2. To make practical suggestions for ensuring gospel-centered churches

SCRIPTURE READING

For our sake he made him to be sin who knew no sin, so that in him we might become the righteousness of God.

—2 Corinthians 5:21

LECTURE OUTLINE

A. The gospel is and must remain at the center of Scripture.
   1. The gospel is the headline of the Bible.
      a. The Old Testament points forward to the gospel, and the Gospels proclaim it.
      b. The rest of the Bible traces out its work in the church.

B. The gospel must be at the center of our faith.
   1. The gospel can be summarized in four words: God, man, Christ, response.
      a. God is holy and loving.
      b. Man sinned and earned the judgment of a holy and loving God.

            c. Christ lived and died in our place to defeat sin and death.
            d. We are called to respond in repentance and faith.
        2. The gospel of Jesus Christ is good news unto salvation.
            a. The gospel is not a message of health and wealth, a message merely proclaiming, "God is love," or a message of Jesus' friendship.
            b. The gospel is a message about a holy and loving God who has made a way for us to be forgiven of our sin and must be heard, believed, and confessed (Rom. 10:9, 17).

    C. The gospel must be at the center of our response to false gospels.
        1. The belief that we must contribute something in order to be saved challenges the gospel.
            a. The gospel is not about enabling us to do good works so that we may be saved by them.
            b. The gospel is the announcement of what Christ has done; we are saved by grace alone through faith alone (Rom. 3:28).
        2. Easy believism is a challenge to the gospel.
            a. The gospel is not a form of Christian nominalism in which we are Christians in name only by virtue of merely assenting to its truths.
            b. Jesus is both Savior and Lord, and in being born of Him, we are new creatures with new desires to obey Him (John 14:15).
        3. Liberal Christianity is a challenge to the gospel.
            a. Liberal Christianity downplays Christ's priestly work in favor of His kingly work, fashioning a Jesus that is Lord but not Savior.
            b. Liberal Christianity emphasizes societal transformation through caring for the needs of the poor and seeking global justice.
            c. We cannot resuscitate society in our own strength; we are bent, broken, and guilty—in need of Christ, our priest and sacrifice.
            d. Prosperity theology is closely related to liberal Christianity, because both make the gospel about the here and now.
        4. Cultural relevance is a challenge to the gospel.
            a. The incarnation of Jesus is often used to prove how the church needs to be culturally relevant "to meet people where they are."
            b. A pragmatic impulse to make the gospel relevant softens it by not mentioning doctrines such as sin, hell, and judgment.
            c. Paul understood the importance of knowing your audience, but he did not hide the offense of the gospel (Acts 17).
            d. An incentivized, watered-down gospel will only give people a weak grasp of the gospel, which leaves them dead in their sin.

    D. The gospel must be at the center of our churches.
        1. A healthy church centers on the gospel; therefore, healthy churches preach the gospel.

a. Join a church where the gospel is preached every Sunday.
b. Pastors, preach the gospel every Sunday.
2. A healthy church centers on the gospel; therefore, healthy churches ensure that members know the gospel.
   a. People must be asked about their understanding of Jesus Christ and the gospel.
   b. People should be able to explain the gospel for their own sake and for the sake of others.
3. A healthy church centers on the gospel; therefore, healthy churches sing and pray the gospel.
   a. The gospel should be a part of our songs: "When I survey the wondrous cross on which the Prince of glory died."
   b. The gospel should be part of our prayers—prayers of intercession, confession, thanksgiving, and praise.
4. A healthy church centers on the gospel; therefore, healthy churches build relationships around the gospel.
   a. The gospel breaks down barriers between people as a display of its power.
   b. A healthy church should be characterized by fellowship between all types of people looking to encourage one another with the gospel.

STUDY QUESTIONS

1. The gospel only faces threats from outside the church.
   a. True
   b. False

2. Easy believism is characteristic of _____.
   a. Orthodox Christianity
   b. Nominal Christianity
   c. Liberal Christianity
   d. None of the above

3. Christian liberalism emphasizes Christ's _____ work over His _____ work.
   a. Priestly; kingly
   b. Priestly; prophetic
   c. Kingly; prophetic
   d. Kingly; priestly

4. The prosperity gospel is not related to liberal Christianity.
   a. True
   b. False

5. The _____ is often used to support the need for the church to be culturally relevant.
   a. Transfiguration
   b. Resurrection
   c. Incarnation
   d. Atonement

6. The gospel is the _____ of the Bible.
   a. Conclusion
   b. Postscript
   c. Footnote
   d. Headline

DISCUSSION QUESTIONS

1. How is the gospel at the center of Scripture, the center of our faith, and the center of a healthy church?

2. What are the characteristics of those who acknowledge Jesus as Savior but not as Lord? What about those who consider Him Lord but not Savior?

3. In what ways are the prosperity gospel and liberal Christianity similar to one another?

4. Paul rebuked Peter for breaking fellowship with the Gentiles (Gal. 2:11–14). What does this tell us about the gospel?

5

Conversion

INTRODUCTION

The health of a church can be measured by its understanding of conversion, as it flows naturally from a right understanding of the gospel. In this lesson, Dr. Dever discusses how biblical conversion is possible and why it is necessary.

LESSON OBJECTIVES

1. To define conversion and how it contributes to the health of a church
2. To answer questions about the possibility and necessity of conversion

SCRIPTURE READING

And calling him a child, he put him in the midst of them and said, "Truly, I say to you, unless you turn and become like children, you will never enter the kingdom of heaven."

—Matthew 18:2–3

LECTURE OUTLINE

A. A biblical understanding of conversion is a mark of a healthy church, yet the need for and possibility of conversion is often looked on with suspicion outside of the church.

1. People are skeptical that change is possible.
   a. People have come to believe that personality and the various vices that go along with it are entirely fixed.
   b. People have come to believe that maturity is the ability to accept and adapt to our fixed internal circumstances.

2. Conversion seems suspicious to those who subscribe to a deterministic worldview.
    a. Offering a hope that change is possible seems manipulative in a society that insists that we only need to embrace who we are.
    b. Offering a hope that change is possible seems to be an invitation to self-hatred.
3. Despite this, people have a deep longing for change.
    a. Work, marriage, family, gender, and death become nothing more than choices, and people find themselves hopeless and defeated.
    b. Conversion confronts the feeling of having nowhere left to turn.

B. Conversion is a real change.
   1. Conversion is turning from ourselves to Christ.
       a. Conversion is turning from our self-serving, self-trusting sin to trusting only in Christ to reconcile us to God.
       b. Paul summarizes conversion as repentance toward God and faith in our Lord Jesus Christ (Acts 20:21).
   2. Conversion is God's work, and understanding this is vital for evangelism and the health of the church.
       a. Evangelism that is rooted in an unbiblical understanding of conversion will likely lead to false converts and sick churches.
       b. A biblical understanding of conversion encourages evangelism that trusts in God, whose Word accomplishes His purposes in making true converts and healthy churches (Isa. 55:11).

C. Conversion is a real need.
   1. People reject their need for change, preferring to remain complacent than to respond to the call to repent and believe.
       a. Churches must be clear that the Bible teaches that, by nature, we have a problem.
       b. People are totally depraved—every aspect of their being has been touched by the fall.
   2. People need God—our condition is described in terms of debt, slavery, and death, and no one will be justified apart from Him (Rom. 3:20).
   3. People need to hear sermons that reflect an understanding of these needs.

D. Conversion is good news.
   1. We are in desperate need of God's grace, yet God owes His grace to no one.
   2. An understanding of our predicament and serious conviction of sin is part of conversion.
   3. Conversion is good news because change is possible and found only in God.
       a. We do not change ourselves, but rather renounce our autonomy and acknowledge God.

      b. We recognize our need for forgiveness and God-oriented lives, experiencing both a change of mind and a change of heart.

E. Conversion is resting in Christ.
1. Conversion is relying on Christ and His righteousness.
   a. Conversion is not our own attempt to be justified before God; nothing we do can make us righteous before Him.
   b. Recognizing our sin forces us to recognize that we are desperate apart from Christ.
2. Conversion is true hope in God's work in Jesus Christ—He sought us, lived for us, died for us, rose for us, and poured out His Spirit into our hearts.
3. Reliance on God is the greatest change that takes place in true conversion.
   a. God promised to give us new hearts through His Spirit so that we would repent and believe (Ezek. 11:19–20).
   b. We are able to accept the truths of God because He has given us a new heart, and it was all His work (John 6:44).

F. Conversion is new birth.
1. Jesus gives us a whole new life and taught that our action in conversion must be brought about by God's action.
   a. Joel prophesied great judgment against unbelieving Israelites and yet offered the hope that "everyone who calls on the name of the Lord shall be saved" (Joel 2:32; Rom. 10:13).
   b. An unbeliever would only desire to call upon God because "among the survivors shall be those whom the Lord calls" (Joel 2:32).

G. A biblical understanding of conversion marks a healthy church.
1. A common misunderstanding is that conversion is something we do, but conversion is more than our action alone.
2. True conversion is the heart-transplanting work of God's Spirit, a change that only God can bring about.

STUDY QUESTIONS

1. Being totally depraved means that we are as bad as we could possibly be.
   a. True
   b. False

2. _____ summarized conversion as repentance toward God and faith in our Lord Jesus Christ.
   a. Paul
   b. John
   c. Luke
   d. James

3. People often reject the _____ and the _____ of conversion.
   a. Opportunity; possibility
   b. Opportunity; necessity
   c. Possibility; necessity
   d. None of the above

4. A biblical understanding of conversion says that it is our own doing.
   a. True
   b. False

5. The Bible uses _____ as an image of our natural state.
   a. Debt
   b. Death
   c. Slavery
   d. All of the above

6. True conversion enables us to say with _____, "Against you, you only, have I sinned."
   a. Paul
   b. Peter
   c. David
   d. Moses

DISCUSSION QUESTIONS

1. Where do you see suspicions about conversion arising in our culture?

2. Why is it important that churches have a biblical understanding of conversion?

3. What are the elements of conversion? What accompanies it?

4. How is a biblical understanding of conversion good news?

6

Evangelism

INTRODUCTION

A biblical understanding and practice of evangelism is a distinguishing mark of a healthy church and the great privilege of every Christian on this side of eternity. In this lesson, Dr. Dever defines what evangelism is and what it is not.

LESSON OBJECTIVES

1. To highlight the consistency in the gospel and evangelism
2. To correct common misconceptions of evangelism

SCRIPTURE READING

For we cannot but speak of what we have seen and heard.

—Acts 5:20

LECTURE OUTLINE

A. A biblical understanding and practice of evangelism can be defined by what it is not.
   1. Evangelism is not imposing our beliefs on other people.
      a. Evangelism is not an imposition of personal beliefs on others—the gospel is fact, not belief or mere opinion.
      b. Evangelism is not forcing anyone to become a Christian; it presents the truth, through which God works as He pleases (1 Cor. 3:6).
   2. Evangelism is not a personal testimony.
      a. Personal testimonies tend to neglect the centrality of the gospel.

  b. Personal testimonies can be a part of evangelism, but they must contain the message of the gospel.
 3. Evangelism is not social action.
  a. Social action without evangelism is only focused on humanity; our greatest problems are not horizontal—they are vertical.
  b. The gospel was at the heart of the world missions movement in the nineteenth century, which resulted in true conversions and prospering nations.
  c. Christianity has incredible social impact, but social impact is always secondary to people's becoming Christians through the gospel.
 4. Evangelism is not apologetics.
  a. Apologetics is defending the faith through answering questions and replying to objections people may have about Christianity.
  b. Apologetics is defensive, whereas evangelism is a positive act of telling the good news about Jesus Christ.
 5. Evangelism is not results oriented.
  a. Evangelism must be properly rooted in a biblical understanding of conversion, understanding that conversion is not in our own hands.
  b. Some people do not respond to the gospel, so the correctness of our message is not finally determined by results.
  c. Results-oriented evangelism can turn a well-meaning church into a pragmatic, results-oriented business.
  d. Results-oriented evangelism produces guilt-ridden Christians who blame themselves for unconverted friends or family members.
  e. Evangelism becomes joyful when we understand our ability to be obedient in sharing the gospel.

B. A biblical understanding and practice of evangelism is properly motivated.
 1. Evangelism can be rightly or wrongly motivated.
  a. Evangelism wrongly motivated is selfish, perhaps a means to argue, reinforce beliefs, or merely gain reputation.
  b. Evangelism rightly motivated is unselfish, manifested in obedience and love.
 2. Evangelism should be done with a desire to be obedient to Christ.
  a. Christ commanded us to be obedient to the Great Commission.
  b. The New Testament records the obedience of first-century Christians, the same obedience we are called to today.
 3. Evangelism should be done with a love for the lost.
  a. Paul displayed his love for the lost in his anguish over his Jewish brothers (Rom. 9:1–3).
  b. Jesus displayed His love for the lost in His tears for Jerusalem (Luke 19:41–44).
  c. God displayed His love for the lost by sending His Son (John 3:16).

4. Evangelism should be done out of love for God.
   a. Love for God is the bedrock of evangelism, because it fights against self-centeredness, difficult circumstances, and difficult people.
   b. Love for God protects the integrity of the gospel, because our love for and fear of man tempt us to water down the gospel.
   c. Evangelism rightly motivated desires to see God glorified: "Then you will know that I am the Lord" (Ezek. 36:36).
   d. Evangelism properly motivated turns our lives outwards for others by sharing the good news and walking in accordance with it (1 Peter 2:12).

C. A biblical understanding and practice of evangelism is essential for church health.
   1. Healthy churches are rooted in the God-centered message and motive.
      a. Evangelism should be done with honesty, urgency, and joy; it should be backed up by the Bible and God-glorifying lives.
      b. God will use us; He has used unlikely people like Moses and Paul.
   2. Healthy churches want to put an end to false evangelism.
      a. Evangelism is not concerned with a shallow one-time decision.
      b. Evangelism is not manufactured revivals.
   3. Healthy churches are committed to sharing the vibrant, living gospel.
      a. The gospel is not cold and debilitating—it's a glorious privilege.
      b. The gospel can recapture joy in our fellowship as we pray together and share it with one another.
   4. Healthy churches understand that God is at work in the gospel.
      a. We came to know the Lord Jesus Christ through hearing the gospel from someone, so we must be faithful in sharing it with others.
      b. Evangelism that understands God's sovereign work is joyful, capturing the heart and empowering us to speak joyfully (Matt. 12:34).

STUDY QUESTIONS

1. Effective evangelism can be measured by results.
   a. True
   b. False

2. _____ as evangelism may never truly present the gospel.
   a. Apologetics
   b. Social action
   c. Personal testimony
   d. All of the above

3. A false motive for evangelism is love for _____.
   a. Obedience
   b. Reputation
   c. Neighbor
   d. Christ

4. Revivals are the key to evangelism and church growth.
    a. True
    b. False

5. Martyn Lloyd-Jones said, "Love for _____ is the only sufficient motive for evangelism."
    a. God
    b. Christ
    c. Neighbor
    d. All of the above

6. Guilt-ridden, joyless evangelism focuses on _____.
    a. Personal testimony
    b. Apologetics
    c. Results
    d. God

DISCUSSION QUESTIONS

1. What are some common misconceptions about evangelism? How are they challenged by the proper motivations for evangelism?

2. What does the impact of nineteenth-century evangelicalism and world missions tell us about the relationship of the gospel to social action?

3. How can you help someone who feels guilty about his or her ineffective evangelism?

4. What does evangelism look like in a healthy church?

7

Membership

INTRODUCTION

Membership in a local church is a prerequisite for fulfilling our obligations to one another. In this lesson, Dr. Leeman defines church membership and connects it to the responsibility of the individual and the church to all that God commands.

LESSON OBJECTIVES

1. To prove church membership from the Bible
2. To define church membership and explain why it matters

SCRIPTURE READING

And they devoted themselves to the apostles' teaching and the fellowship, to the breaking of bread and the prayers.

—Acts 2:42

Bear one another's burdens, and so fulfill the law of Christ.

—Galatians 6:2

LECTURE OUTLINE

A. Church membership is in the Bible.
  1. The Bible speaks clearly about church membership.
     a. The church discipline passages of Matthew 18 and 1 Corinthians 5 prove the reality of church membership.

b. Church membership must first exist in order for someone to be removed from it.
2. Church membership needs to be understood in light of what the Bible says about the church.
   a. The church is described as the family of God, so membership in a local church looks like membership in a family (1 Tim. 5:1–2).
   b. The church is described as a holy nation, so membership in a local church resembles citizenship; we are called to submit to our leaders and to one another as members of the kingdom.
   c. The church is described as the body of Christ, so membership involves dependence on one another (1 Cor. 12:21–26).
   d. There are more than ninety metaphors describing the church: flock, temple, people, vine, pillar and buttress of truth, lady and her children, etc.

B. Church membership is an individual and corporate necessity.
   1. Anti-institutional sentimentality leads people astray.
      a. Being a member of a local church is an essential part of being a member of the body of Christ.
      b. The idea of a Christian who does not submit to a church is foreign to the Bible.
   2. Church membership is required for obedience to all the Bible commands.
      a. Christians are called to submit to their leaders (Heb. 13:17).
      b. Christians are called to build one another up by speaking the truth in love (Eph. 4:15–16).
      c. Christians are called to submit to one another and address each other in psalms, hymns, and spiritual songs (Eph. 5:19–21).
   3. Church membership is required for a church to exercise authority.
      a. The church exercises authority by bringing people into membership through baptism, which identifies them with Christ.
      b. The church exercises authority by affirming members through the Lord's Supper, identifying all those who partake of the one bread as one body (1 Cor. 10:17).
      c. The church exercises authority by disciplining members through excommunication in severe cases of unrepentant sin.
   4. Christians cannot exist as the body of Christ apart from a self-conscious commitment to a local church.
      a. Church membership is the only way to fulfill all the Bible's commands about life together.
      b. Church membership is the only way for the church to respond to the authority given to it by the Word to announce who is in the church.
   5. The authority of the church to declare to the world who is identified with Christ is rooted in Scripture.
      a. Jeremiah and Ezekiel promised a new covenant wherein God would place His law on people's hearts and forgive their sins but did not answer how we will know who the people of the new covenant are.

- b. The work of the Holy Spirit in conversion is an invisible work, so the invisible community of the church must become visible.
- c. Jesus gave the Apostles and the church the keys of the kingdom for binding and loosing, which they exercised through baptism and the Lord's Supper.
- d. The relationship of justification and sanctification is analogous to the church: you prove that you belong to Christ by belonging to a church.
- e. Christians in the New Testament are united together as the church, loving one another as they loved God (1 John 4:20–21).

C. Church membership is defined as a church's formal affirmation and oversight of an individual's submission to a local body of believers.
  1. The church affirms a believer's profession of faith and oversees a believer's discipleship to Christ while the believer commits to growing in Christ, being discipled inside of a church's affirmation and oversight.
  2. The relationship between the church and a believer implies that they know one another.
     a. A church should know what its potential members believe, and potential members should know what the church believes.
     b. This basic principle can be seen in the exchange between Jesus and Peter: "But who do you say that I am?" (Luke 9:20).
     c. Church membership classes and membership interviews should establish a conversation between the believer and the church.
  3. Church membership is how a line is kept between the church and the world.
     a. Contemporary sensibilities make Christians uncomfortable with this idea, but the people of God have always been distinguishable.
     b. Keeping the line between the church and the world clear is a powerful witness that God really does save people, calling them to live as salt and light (Matt. 5:13–16).
  4. Church membership in a healthy church will reflect the very same metaphors the Bible uses of the church.
     a. Church membership in the healthy life of a church should resemble the everyday gospel-centered lives of Christians living for each other.
     b. The first-century church is a perfect example of the fellowship that church membership provides (Acts 2:42–47).
     c. Church membership is not a lifeless institution reserved for one day of the week; it is a vital part of the everyday needs of God's people.
  5. Church membership matters.
     a. Church membership is biblical, it creates the church, and it is a prerequisite for the Lord's Table.
     b. Church membership is how we officially represent the King, declare our highest allegiance, and embody and experience the biblical metaphors for the church.

c. Church membership is how we serve other Christians, follow other Christians, and how leaders lead other Christians.
d. Church membership is what makes church discipline possible, structuring our lives and building a witness that invites the nations.

STUDY QUESTIONS

1. Church membership and obedience are unrelated.
    a. True
    b. False

2. The church as _____ is not a metaphor used in the Bible.
    a. Body
    b. Bread
    c. Temple
    d. Flock

3. Announcing that you belong to Christ through church membership is similar to the relationship between _____ and _____.
    a. Election; adoption
    b. Atonement; expiation
    c. Satisfaction; propitiation
    d. Justification; sanctification

4. Church membership is an essential part of identifying the people of God.
    a. True
    b. False

5. Church membership is required for a church's _____.
    a. Growth
    b. Oversight
    c. Profession
    d. All of the above

6. Church membership is required for a believer's _____.
    a. Growth
    b. Oversight
    c. Affirmation
    d. None of the above

DISCUSSION QUESTIONS

1. How would you prove to someone from the Bible that church membership is necessary?

2. What metaphors for the church do you think are the strongest? Why?

3. Why does our culture fight against the concept of church membership?

4. Dr. Leeman gave many examples of what church membership looks like in a healthy church. What are some similar examples from your own church?

8

Discipline

INTRODUCTION

Church discipline is not popular, but it is nonetheless a necessary dimension of a church's faithfulness to God and His people. In this lesson, Dr. Leeman defines church discipline and how it is a necessary and loving mark of a healthy church.

LESSON OBJECTIVES

1. To define church discipline and how it should look in the local church
2. To establish the loving character of biblical church discipline

SCRIPTURE READING

For such a one, this punishment by the majority is enough, so you should rather turn to forgive and comfort him, or he may be overwhelmed by excessive sorrow. So I beg you to reaffirm your love for him.

—2 Corinthians 2:7–8

LECTURE OUTLINE

A. What does the Bible say about church discipline?
  1. Jesus tells the church to practice discipline in matters of unrepented sin.
     a. We are to approach others about sin individually, and if they do not listen, we approach them in the company of two or three witnesses.
     b. If they do not listen and refuse to repent, we approach them with the church, and if they do not listen to the church, we are to treat them as unbelievers (Matt. 18:15–20).

c. Jesus is concerned to resolve cases of unrepented sin between two people but is also willing to bring cases before the church.
2. Paul tells the church to practice discipline in matters of unrepented sin.
a. Paul is confronting a church for tolerating a man who is sleeping with his stepmother, a man who is presumably unrepentant.
b. Paul commands the church to hand him over to Satan for his refusal to repent, declaring him a citizen of the kingdom of the world.
c. Paul concludes this account by asserting the responsibility of the church to judge its own (1 Cor. 5).

B. What is church discipline?
1. Church discipline is an aspect of Christian discipleship.
a. *Discipline* and *disciple* are etymologically related, both taken from the realm of education, which involves teaching and correction.
b. Two types of discipline: formative discipline is teaching through forming, and corrective discipline is teaching through correction.
c. Discipline involves growth, so making disciples involves teaching and correction.
2. Church discipline is the formal public act of excluding a professed Christian from church membership and the Lord's Table for serious, unrepented sin.
a. This is the practice of excommunication, an act whereby a church announces that it can no longer affirm a profession of faith.
b. Church discipline is not an act of retribution; it is a loving act intended to remedy someone's sin, "so that his spirit may be saved in the day of the Lord" (1 Cor. 5:5).
c. From the perspective of those who believe in a final judgment, church discipline is the most loving way to warn an unrepentant sinner.

C. Is church discipline loving?
1. The Bible defines love in terms of obedience, and the Lord disciplines those He loves (John 14:20–23, 15:10–11; Heb. 12:8; 1 John 5:3).
2. A church disciplines for the sake of the individual, the congregation, the non-Christian neighbor, and the name of Christ.

D. What are the results of church discipline?
1. Church discipline grows the church in love and holiness.
a. Hebrews 12:11 describes it as the "peaceful fruit of righteousness."
b. While discipline may be scorned, members of the church grow in their desire for the purity and peace of the church.
2. Church discipline is a compelling witness to the world.
a. The church is contrasted with the rest of society (1 Peter 2:11–12).
b. The church will cause the nations to praise God through its reverence for His holiness.

E. Which sins require church discipline?
   1. A sin must have an outward manifestation—a mere suspicion of pride or greed does not lead to formal discipline.
   2. A sin must be serious—a brother who exaggerates the details of a story should not be exposed to formal, public exclusion.
   3. A sin must be unrepented sin—if someone is refusing to be obedient to God's commands, he is prizing his sin more than he prizes Jesus.

F. How quickly should a church act?
   1. Sometimes church discipline should be a slow process.
      a. Everyone sins differently and should be approached differently (1 Thess. 5:14).
      b. Repentance may be present and should be identified (Isa. 42:3).
   2. Sometimes, church discipline must be swift in cases of unabashed sin.

G. How should we interact with someone who has been disciplined?
   1. The family is a different institution than the church, so family members must still maintain biblical family obligations.
   2. The Lord's Supper should not be taken with disciplined members, and the tenor of interactions with them should change.
   3. The hope is that disciplined members continue to attend worship to hear the gospel even when the hand of fellowship is no longer extended.

H. When should a church restore someone from discipline?
   1. Restoration to fellowship occurs when there is repentance, and the character of repentance is dependent on the nature of the sin.
   2. Restoration to fellowship does not accompany a probationary period but restoration to full-fledged fellowship.
   3. Restoration to fellowship accompanies a church's public announcement of forgiveness and affirmation of love for the repenting individual.
   4. Restoration to fellowship is an occasion for any church to celebrate.

STUDY QUESTIONS

1. Church discipline begins by confronting sin with a group of elders.
   a. True
   b. False

2. Church discipline is a form of _____ discipline.
   a. Formative
   b. Corrective
   c. Permissive
   d. Authoritative

3. Church discipline is for the sake of the _____.
   a. Church
   b. Individual
   c. Name of Christ
   d. All of the above

4. Restoration to fellowship is accompanied by a probationary period.
   a. True
   b. False

5. Love is marked by _____.
   a. Approval
   b. Tolerance
   c. Obedience
   d. Acceptance

6. Church discipline is for matters of _____ sin.
   a. Venial
   b. Formal
   c. Internal
   d. Unrepented

DISCUSSION QUESTIONS

1. Church discipline is often stigmatized as harsh and unloving. How would you convince someone that church discipline is actually an act of love?

2. Why do you think repentance is such a central concern for restoration to fellowship?

3. Why is it important to confront someone who has refused to repent of his or her sin against you in the presence of two or three witnesses?

4. Why is church discipline a mark of a healthy church? What does the mere presence of church discipline tell you about the individual believers within a church?

9

Discipleship & Growth

INTRODUCTION

The local church is essential for Christian discipleship—growing in Christ and helping others to grow in Christ. In this lesson, Dr. Dever covers the role of the pastor, congregation, and individual for discipleship in a healthy church.

LESSON OBJECTIVES

1. To clarify the difference between discipleship and discipling
2. To describe the responsibilities of the pastor, congregation, and individual to one another in discipleship

SCRIPTURE READING

Iron sharpens iron, and one man sharpens another.

—Proverbs 27:17

Therefore be imitators of God, as beloved children.

—Ephesians 5:1

LECTURE OUTLINE

A. The local church is the incubator of our spiritual growth.
   1. Discipleship and discipling go hand in hand.
      a. Discipleship is the process of following Christ.
      b. Discipling is the process of helping others follow Christ.
      c. Discipleship cannot be done without discipling.

2. A healthy church is filled with people who follow Christ and help others follow Christ—this is the model of the New Testament church (2 Tim. 2:2).

B. The local church is the pastor's natural arena for discipleship.
   1. Pastors disciple people with the Word of God.
      a. The Word is as central in the work of a pastor as it is in the work of the Spirit at conversion (Acts 2, 10; Rom. 10:17; Ezek. 37).
      b. The Word is our sustenance, and God equips Christians through those He has gifted to teach it (Deut. 8:3).
      c. Jesus taught with the Word and the disciples taught with the Word, understanding its role in teaching and training men.
   2. Pastors cultivate an environment for discipleship to flourish.
      a. Discipleship is publicly proclaimed in baptism and the celebration of the Lord's Supper.
      b. Discipleship is done on a ground level through church membership, pastoral care, and church discipline.
   3. Pastors are called to provide an example.
      a. Paul appealed to his own example (1 Cor. 11:1; Phil. 3:17).
      b. In the same way, a pastor's life should be an example particularly for those they are called to shepherd (Heb. 13:7, 17).
   4. Pastors must give an account one day.
      a. Pastors must give an account for their teaching (James 3:1).
      b. Pastors must give an account for their people (Heb. 13:17).
      c. Pastors must make decisions about doctrine and membership while counseling individuals from the Word, praying for their congregations, and ensuring that people are being equipped to grow in Christ.

C. The local church is the congregation's natural arena for discipleship.
   1. Congregations have a responsibility to the work of their pastors.
      a. A congregation must acknowledge its elders as gifts from Christ to the church.
      b. God accomplishes the mission of the church through a congregation's prayers and support of its pastors and the work of the ministry.
   2. Congregations should pray for and pay their pastors.
      a. Prayer is foundational to the work of the local church; the New Testament is filled with requests for prayers (Heb. 13:18).
      b. Pastors who labor in preaching and teaching should be paid so that they can devote themselves to the ministry (1 Tim. 5:17).
   3. Congregations must hold teachers accountable.
      a. Congregations must be willing to reject false teachers, working to remove pastors who are not faithful to the gospel (Gal. 1:8).
      b. Congregations that remove false teachers actually spare them from greater judgment (James 3:1).

c. Congregations that allow serious false teaching are responsible for it (2 Tim. 4:3–4).
d. Congregations must seek teachers who are faithful to the Word of God so that they will know the will of God.
4. Congregations have a responsibility to love one another, stirring one another up to love and good works (Heb. 10:24).

D. The local church is the individual's natural arena for discipleship.
1. Individuals have a responsibility to the congregation as a whole.
   a. Individuals need to be respectful of the congregation's stewardship.
   b. Individuals do this by praying for others, loving others, and counseling others; we must read Scripture and trustworthy books so that we may help others grow in Christ.
2. Knit with the congregation and pastor in an environment of discipleship and growth, individuals play an important role in making a healthy church.

STUDY QUESTIONS

1. Pastors lead the local church through preaching and teaching only.
   a. True
   b. False

2. *Pastor* can be used interchangeably with _____.
   a. Elder
   b. Deacon
   c. Apostle
   d. Evangelist

3. The gifts of a pastor are particularly important to the life of the church because they are intimately connected to the _____.
   a. Word
   b. Pulpit
   c. Congregation
   d. All of the above

4. A congregation shares in the blame for false teaching.
   a. True
   b. False

5. A congregation has a duty to remove a pastor who teaches false doctrine for the sake of the _____.
   a. Pastor
   b. Individual
   c. Congregation
   d. All of the above

6. A culture of discipleship and growth in a healthy local church depends on the
   _____.
   a. Pastor
   b. Individual
   c. Congregation
   d. All of the above

DISCUSSION QUESTIONS

1. Why is the local church such an essential part of our Christian growth? How does our own growth relate to the growth of other Christians?

2. What are different responsibilities a congregation bears toward its pastors? What responsibility do you think is the most dangerous if neglected?

3. Some people question whether a pastor should be paid. How would you argue that it is appropriate for a congregation to support its pastor?

4. What are ways you can improve in growing in Christ and in helping others to grow in Christ in your local church?

10

Leadership

INTRODUCTION

Scripture clearly establishes the context and the role of church leadership. In this lesson, Dr. Dever explains how the context of leadership is the congregation and how the role of leadership is the faithful work of elders and deacons.

LESSON OBJECTIVES

1. To describe the role of the congregation in church leadership
2. To outline the qualifications of and differences between elders and deacons

SCRIPTURE READING

Remember your leaders, those who spoke to you the word of God. Consider the outcome of their way of life, and imitate their faith.

—Hebrews 13:7

LECTURE OUTLINE

A. The context for leadership in a healthy local church is the congregation.
   1. The New Testament stresses the congregation's role in the life of the church.
      a. The New Testament is not a straightforward manual of church polity where an ideal constitution and bylaws are presented.
      b. Throughout the centuries, there has been controversy over who God has intended to govern the church.
      c. The congregation plays a very important role in the life of the church regardless of church polity.

2. Matthew 18:15–20 is a passage about the role of the congregation: the congregation rules over escalated disputes over sin (Matt. 18:17).
3. Act 6:1–7 is a passage about the role of the congregation: the congregation chose the first seven deacons of the church.
   a. Using the New Testament as a guide for church government is difficult because of the presence of the Apostles.
   b. Apostles had an authority that no Christian can claim today, yet they still gave the congregation the responsibility of selecting deacons.
   c. The Apostles recognized the authority of the assembly under God in the same way that Jesus taught it in Matthew 18:15–20.
4. Paul's letters are continuations of Jesus' teaching and Apostolic practice that the congregation plays a central role in discipline and doctrine.
   a. Paul rebukes the congregation for not realizing its responsibility to discipline the man who has his father's wife (1 Cor. 5).
   b. Paul remarks on a case of church discipline about the "punishment by the majority," referring to the church members in the majority vote (2 Cor. 2:6).
   c. Paul insists that the congregation judge the content of what is being presented to it as the gospel even from the Apostles (Gal. 1:6–10).
   d. Paul warns the Ephesians about false teachers and the culpability of the congregation for tolerating them (2 Tim. 4:3).
5. Congregations have a responsibility in recovering healthy churches.
   a. Regardless of denomination, congregations are simply the gathered people that together form a church.
   b. Congregations must be involved in the life of the church and must be recognized by the gifted leaders of a congregation, both working together to discern the will of God.
6. Congregations have a responsibility to recognize, trust, and honor those whom God has gifted to lead.
   a. Congregations must cultivate a culture of thankfulness where leaders are honored and esteemed as gifts of Christ to the church (Eph. 4:11).
   b. A leader's untrustworthiness and a congregation's lack of trust are serious deficiencies in a church and are not the biblical model (Heb. 13:17).
   c. Congregations are called to obey and submit to leaders, which requires them to trust imperfect yet qualified men.

B. The role of leadership in a healthy local church is founded on Scripture.
   1. Elders are men given to the work of pastoral oversight and teaching, qualified by their character, spiritual gifts, and pastoral concern.
      a. The two most common names in the New Testament for this office are *episkopos* (overseer) and *presbuteros* (elder).
      b. The New Testament references to elders indicate that there should be a plurality of elders in each local church (Titus 1:5; James 5:14).
      c. The New Testament specifies different elder roles; a preaching pastor is an elder, but not all elders are preaching pastors.

2. A plurality of elders is a benefit to pastors and congregations.
   a. A plurality of elders distributes the pastoral work within the congregation beyond an individual pastor's reach.
   b. A plurality of elders helps to counsel, support, supplement, and protect a pastor when decisions need to be made.
   c. A plurality of elders is an important leadership structure that promotes a church's continued responsibility and growth in spiritual maturity.
3. Deacons are men given to the physical needs of the church, qualified by their character, spiritual gifts, and pastoral concern.
   a. Deacons are concerned for the administration and maintenance of a church and the physical needs of its members.
   b. Deacons work to meet the physical needs of the church in order to free ministers of the Word to meet the spiritual needs of the church.
4. Leaders in the church must meet the qualifications set forth in Scripture.
   a. Leaders will be marked by their character, reputation, and ability to handle the Word, meeting the qualifications in 1 Timothy and Titus.
   b. Leaders will be marked by trustworthiness and a willingness to trust a congregation's decisions and commitments.
   c. Leaders will be marked by an other-centeredness, displaying the true marks of hospitality found in an elder or a deacon.
5. Leadership in the church in both its role and context purely shines the light of the gospel into the world—a mark of a healthy church.

STUDY QUESTIONS

1. The New Testament reads like a straightforward manual for church polity.
   a. True
   b. False

2. Acts 6 serves as an example of the responsibilities of a congregation in church leadership when the congregation chose the _____.
   a. Pastor
   b. Elders
   c. Deacons
   d. Apostles

3. The New Testament teaches the need for a _____ of elders.
   a. Majority
   b. Plurality
   c. Diversity
   d. Disparity

4. A church model where a congregation is responsible for doctrine and discipline is only possible in congregationalism.
   a. True
   b. False

5. *Plenum* is the Greek word used in 2 Corinthians 2:6 for _____.
   a. "Plenty"
   b. "Minority"
   c. "Majority"
   d. "Congregation"

6. *Elder* can be used interchangeably with _____.
   a. Apostle
   b. Deacon
   c. Prophet
   d. Overseer

DISCUSSION QUESTIONS

1. How does the New Testament assert the role of the congregation in the leadership of the church?

2. Dr. Dever mentioned a church's need for a right balance of trust and authority. What does that right balance look like in a local church?

3. What are the benefits of a plurality of elders to the local church for pastors and congregations?

4. What are some primary concerns behind the qualifications for leaders and the responsibilities of a congregation?

11

Corporate Prayer

INTRODUCTION

Prayer is central to the Christian life, so it is no surprise that it is also central in a healthy church. In this lesson, Dr. Dever illustrates the prayer life of a healthy church while emphasizing the content, context, purpose, and power of prayer.

LESSON OBJECTIVES

1. To describe the character of public prayer in a healthy church
2. To categorize the content and variety of prayer beneficial to a local church

SCRIPTURE READING

Rejoice in hope, be patient in tribulation, be constant in prayer.

—Romans 12:12

LECTURE OUTLINE

A. All of our public prayer as a church should be an outgrowth of our private prayer.
   1. The New Testament commands us to pray without ceasing (1 Thess. 5:17).
      a. A pattern for prayer is established in a variety of circumstances that support the possibility of continuous prayer.
      b. Praying without ceasing means that Christians must pray privately.
   2. All basic aspects of prayer should be in our personal prayer time—praise, thanksgiving, confession, intercession, and supplication.

B. A church's practice of prayer will vary because there is a natural liberty in prayer.
   1. There is no set time for church prayer meetings; a church may meet on a Sunday or on a Wednesday or have a prayer time for specific demographics.
   2. A church may decide to meet in response to events in the life of the church or in the life of the nation, giving itself to prayer for God's work around the world.

C. Specific language is helpful in leading a church in prayer.
   1. The church is one body, so representative prayer uses plural pronouns.
      a. Jesus taught us to pray, "Our Father" (Matt. 6:9–13).
      b. Public prayer is an opportunity to lead the church into the presence of God, acting as a representative for one people.
      c. The natural focus of public prayer is on matters of common concern.
   2. The church is one body, so it identifies and agrees with representative prayer.
      a. A congregation should say, "Amen," at the conclusion of prayers as a verbalized agreement and ownership of what has been prayed.
      b. "Amen" is rooted in the Hebrew word for "this is true" or "I agree."
   3. The church is one body, so the language used in prayer communicates the unity found among one people coming before God.

D. Different types of public prayer help a local church.
   1. A church may have a combination of short and long, spontaneous and planned prayers, each serving a particular function within the church.
      a. Prepared prayers are important considering the representative nature of public prayer.
      b. People often equate spontaneity with sincerity, but prayers that are thought out beforehand are not necessarily insincere.
      c. Short prayers take less time to prepare and are inherently flexible, so a church can pray for a variety of matters over a brief period of time.

E. Prayers on the Lord's Day should be specifically directed toward praising God.
   1. The Bible gives us examples of prayers of praise.
      a. Jesus taught us to pray, "Hallowed be your name" (Matt. 6:9–13).
      b. David extols and commends God by reflecting on His grace, mercy, and goodness in Psalm 145.
   2. Prayers of praise will help a church think about God throughout the week as the self-existing, ever-present, Almighty God of goodness, mercy, and love.
   3. Prayers of praise can be supplemented with thanksgiving.
      a. We thank God for what He has done (Rev. 4:11).
      b. When the disciples gather to pray in Acts 4:23–31, their requests are overshadowed by praise.

F. Prayers on the Lord's Day should be specifically directed toward confession to God.
   1. The Bible gives us examples of prayers of confession.
      a. Jesus taught us to pray, "Forgive us our debts" (Matt. 6:9–13).
      b. The Psalms are filled with prayers of confession (Ps. 32:5), and the Bible commands us to confess our sins (James 5:16; 1 John 1:9).
   2. Confession is the continual practice of acknowledging the truth of God.
      a. Christians are forgiven and yet continue to confess their sins to God because the daily nature of the Christian life is repentance and faith.
      b. Confession is publically declaring that God is true, we have sinned against Him, and we need Jesus Christ.
      c. Confession highlights the gospel of a holy God who lovingly receives our confession because of the person and work of His very own Son.
      d. Confession exalts the mercy of God and gives us an opportunity to marvel at His wondrous love.

G. Prayers on the Lord's Day should be dedicated to asking for God's help.
   1. Jesus taught us to pray, "Your kingdom come" and "Give us this day our daily bread" (Matt. 6:9–13).
   2. Pastoral prayers may vary by context but should contain essential categories.
      a. Prayers should represent those present in particular times of need or who sense their own need.
      b. Prayers should resemble the concerns of the sermon and should be offered for governing authorities (1 Tim. 2:1–2).
      c. Prayers should be made for other denominations, the preaching of the gospel, and our persecuted brothers and sisters around the world.

H. Prayer should characterize the life of the church, and the entire congregation should meet for prayer.
   1. Prayer should characterize more than just worship by being a regular part of the meetings and daily interactions within a church.
   2. The life of a local church involves prayer, so doing the beneficial spiritual work of prayer should be commonplace for every member within a church.

STUDY QUESTIONS

1. Prayer meetings should be at the same time at all churches.
   a. True
   b. False

2. Christians are to say, _____, which means, "This is true."
   a. "Selah"
   b. "Amen"
   c. "Hallelujah"
   d. "Maranatha"

11—Corporate Prayer

3. Dr. Dever mentioned extended sessions of prayer that lasted hours at a time during the _____.
   a. Constitutional Convention
   b. First General Assembly
   c. Westminster Assembly
   d. Synod of Dort

4. Public prayers that are prepared beforehand are typically insincere.
   a. True
   b. False

5. We publicly acknowledge the righteousness of God's disputes with us during prayers of _____.
   a. Praise
   b. Confession
   c. Supplication
   d. Thanksgiving

6. The prayer of the disciples in Acts 4 demonstrates the priority of _____ even when the purpose of our prayer is to bring a request before God.
   a. Praise
   b. Confession
   c. Supplication
   d. All of the above

DISCUSSION QUESTIONS

1. Paul exhorts us to pray without ceasing (1 Thess. 5:17). How does a Christian's liberty in prayer make this possible?

2. What elements should be present in our personal and corporate prayers? Is there a particular element you would like to focus on improving in your own prayer life?

3. How could you convince someone that Christians, though forgiven, should confess their sins before God? Why is confession such a blessing for Christians?

4. Why is prayer for civil magistrates and the church worldwide important? What does it demonstrate about the Christian faith?

12

The Great Commission

INTRODUCTION

He who has been given all authority in heaven and on earth has commissioned us. In this lesson, Dr. Dever shows that God established the church so that we might fulfill this Great Commission.

LESSON OBJECTIVES

1. To elaborate on how we are to fulfill the Great Commission
2. To situate the Great Commission in the greater context of the Bible

SCRIPTURE READING

Go therefore and make disciples of all nations, baptizing them in the name of the Father and of the Son and of the Holy Spirit, teaching them to observe all that I have commanded you.

—Matthew 28:19–20a

LECTURE OUTLINE

A. How are we to fulfill the Great Commission?
  1. There is one imperative in the Great Commission: "Make disciples."
     a. The imperative verb "make disciples" is one word in the Greek.
     b. There is a participle, "Go," which, coming before the imperative, has a special emphasis; the others are "baptizing" and "teaching."
  2. Christians are to go to all the nations as part of God's unfolding mission.
     a. Jesus first sent His disciples to the lost sheep of Israel (Matt. 10:6).

  b. Jesus next sends His disciples to all the nations as part of His always-intended mission to bless them.
 3. The local church is the means God has given us to fulfill His commands.
  a. Church-less evangelism leaves new converts helpless and exposed.
  b. Converts must be incorporated into a biblically faithful church marked by gospel preaching and the right administration of the sacraments.

B. What's the big picture of the Great Commission?
 1. God desires a fatherly relationship with His people.
  a. God created our first parents and is naturally concerned with us as their children; our interrelatedness reflects God's triunity.
  b. God's pattern of working corporately with people extends into the New Testament as God fulfills His promise of blessing the nations.
  c. The Bible unfolds the story of God's faithfulness to His promise such that all of history culminates in a corporate expression (Rev. 7:9).
  d. People were created to be in relationship with God, and the Bible tells the story about how God is reestablishing this relationship.

C. What has God done for the Great Commission?
 1. Jesus' ministry follows the pattern of God's relational design for us.
  a. God loved us and designed us for relationship, so it is not surprising that Jesus summarized the law as love for God and love for neighbor.
  b. Love is foundational to how we are to relate to God and neighbor and is the distinguishing mark of Christ's disciples (John 13:35).
 2. Jesus established the church as the continuing work of His Father.
  a. Jesus established the church with His authority over all things.
  b. Jesus entrusted the church with His authority to proclaim His message and lead His people.
 3. The Father, Son, and Holy Spirit created the church to fulfill the work of the Great Commission.
  a. The church is the household of God paid for with His own blood (Acts 20:28; 1 Tim. 3:15).
  b. God established, sustains, and equips the church for His purposes.

D. What did the Apostles understand by the Great Commission?
 1. The Apostles established and cared for churches.
  a. The Apostles planted churches in Jerusalem and Antioch, and Paul eventually commissioned churches among the Gentiles.
  b. Churches were strengthened and grew in number, meeting regularly on the Lord's Day.
  c. The Apostles' establishment of and care for churches was the only way to be obedient to the Great Commission.
 2. The Apostles taught concerning our responsibility to each other within the church.
  a. We are called to guide, admonish, and edify one another.

b. We are called to safeguard the gospel against false teachers.
  c. We are obedient to the Great Commission through the local church.
 3. The Apostles' response to the Great Commission teaches us that the church was established for more than mere decisions for Christ.
    a. Jesus wants disciples, not decisions.
    b. The only way we can be obedient to the Bible's commands is through a self-conscious commitment to our discipleship in a local church.

E. What is our goal in fulfilling the Great Commission?
 1. Our goal is God's glory.
    a. Christ identifies with the church so we are to reflect His love and wisdom as a display of His power (Eph. 3:10; Col. 1:18; 1 John 4:20).
    b. The church is the visible display of the gospel in the world, the means by which the world will see God's power in a community of people made in His image and reborn by His Spirit.

STUDY QUESTIONS

1. Jesus' command that we go to all the nations was an unforeseen event in redemptive history.
   a. True
   b. False

2. In the Greek, the one imperative verb in the Great Commission is _____.
   a. "Go"
   b. "Baptize"
   c. "Teach"
   d. "Make disciples"

3. Our relational nature reflects God's _____.
   a. Aseity
   b. Triunity
   c. Eternality
   d. Immutability

4. The Great Commission is fulfilled primarily through individual evangelism.
   a. True
   b. False

5. The first local church that resulted from the day of Pentecost was the church in _____.
   a. Syria
   b. Cilicia
   c. Antioch
   d. Jerusalem

6. The church is meant to display God's _____.
    a. Glory
    b. Gospel
    c. Character
    d. All of the above

DISCUSSION QUESTIONS

1. Why is the church an essential aspect of evangelism? How essential has the church been for your growth in grace?

2. Throughout the Bible, God initiates relationships with His people. How does this help you understand your role in the Great Commission?

3. In what ways are you challenged by the Apostles' understanding of the Great Commission, especially in regard to the responsibilities they gave to every believer in the church?

4. How is a low view of the church detrimental to believers and unbelievers?

13

Missions

INTRODUCTION

History is a tale of God's mission of reconciling the world to Himself. In this lesson, Dr. Dever shares what a great privilege it is to be a part of God's mission to the nations, an essential concern and mark of a healthy church.

LESSON OBJECTIVES

1. To demonstrate how the beliefs of a church influence world missions
2. To demonstrate how the actions of a church influence world missions

SCRIPTURE READING

You will be my witnesses in Jerusalem and in all Judea and Samaria, and to the end of the earth.

—Acts 1:8b

And how are they to hear without someone preaching?

—Romans 10:14b

LECTURE OUTLINE

A. A biblical understanding of missions in the life of a local church depends on what a local church believes.
   1. Missions is evangelism across borders, particularly across language barriers.
      a. It is the biblical concept of sharing the gospel in a place and among a people where it is largely unknown.

b. The mission of missions is gospel transformation—the transformation of the nature of humanity and reconciliation with God.
   2. The basic story of the Bible is God's mission of reconciliation.
      a. God promises redemption to Adam and Eve and promises Abram a nation that will in turn bless all the earth (Gen. 3, 12).
      b. God is faithful to His promises and delivers Israel from the hands of the Egyptians, always intending to bless the nations through them.
      c. God fulfills His promises through His Servant Jesus Christ who in turn sends His disciples to all the nations (Isa. 49:6).
   3. The gospel of Jesus Christ is at the heart of the faith.
      a. The gospel is the only means by which God is reconciling the world to Himself and so must never be changed (Gal. 1:8).
      b. The gospel is at the center of a healthy church because it is the only way people may turn from darkness to light (Acts 26:16–18).
   4. The gospel is the seed of missions in the church.
      a. Gospel faith accompanies repentance, so true Christianity has a quality of self-denial that leads us to take up our cross in love.
      b. Gospel self-sacrifice combines with love of God and neighbor for world missions.
   5. Missions begins at home through evangelism and a genuine concern for the conversion of friends and family.
      a. If people are not equipped and encouraged to evangelize at home, they will not be equipped and encouraged to evangelize abroad.
      b. Evangelism on the home front teaches people the basics for world missions, evangelism in a cross-cultural context.
   6. A church that makes evangelism seem optional handicaps world missions.
      a. A concern for missions should accompany a concern for discipling each other in Scripture and holiness.
      b. We participate in the larger story of the Bible by sharing the gospel and showing a concern for people in far-off places.
      c. Evangelism and missions are a natural part of being a God-focused Christian who is concerned for those who do not yet know Him.

B. A biblical understanding of missions in the life of a local church depends on what a local church does.
   1. We learn about God's Word and God's world, becoming a missionary-sending church by preaching the missions-saturated gospel.
   2. We pray for the spread of the Gospel in other parts of the world, asking that we might be a part of God's worldwide work.
   3. We plan to make our church increasingly useful to the spread of the gospel by caring for other churches.
      a. Churches should develop relationships to strengthen one another and nourish new churches.

b. Churches should not be program-driven so that members have time throughout the week to minister to their communities.
4. We support those on mission for the sake of Christ (Titus 3:13; 3 John 5–8).
5. We send pastors to help establish churches in places that need the gospel.
6. We care for those we send by helping them during their transitional stages.
7. We wait for a faithful, well-established witness, helping those we send so that they might endure.

C. A biblical understanding of missions in the life of a local church depends on our desire to see people converted for the glory of God.
  1. Missions is vital because it involves taking the gospel to places where it is largely unknown.
     a. Salvation comes through the ministry of the Word, so people are not saved apart from hearing the gospel (Rom. 10:14; 1 Tim 4:13).
     b. A healthy church that understands this reality will have a biblical understanding and practice of world missions for God's glory.

STUDY QUESTIONS

1. The basic story of the Bible was never merely about an ethnic minority.
   a. True
   b. False

2. Missions is taking the gospel across boundaries, especially across _____ boundaries.
   a. Ethnic
   b. Economic
   c. Language
   d. Geographic

3. God promised to bless the nations through _____.
   a. Israel
   b. Jesus
   c. Abraham
   d. All of the above

4. Missions is an aspect of evangelism.
   a. True
   b. False

5. It is in the combination of _____ and love of God and neighbor that we find the seed of missions in the church.
   a. Faith
   b. Justice

c. Courage
   d. Self-sacrifice

6. A narrative with a strong emphasis on missions can especially be found in _____.
   a. Revelation
   b. Exodus
   c. Joshua
   d. Acts

DISCUSSION QUESTIONS

1. Why do you think everyday evangelism cultivates a culture of missions?

2. How can you trace God's missionary intent throughout the Bible? How is evangelism participating in the same overarching narrative?

3. What must a healthy church do to promote the spread of the gospel?

4. What is your specific prayer for missionaries, evangelists, and those who are suffering persecution in the church worldwide?

14

Raising Up Leaders

INTRODUCTION

The faith once delivered to the saints must be handed down from generation to generation. In this lesson, Dr. Dever offers nine marks for identifying, growing, and training elders for the sake of a healthy church.

LESSON OBJECTIVES

1. To identify the traits of the men God is raising up for leadership
2. To suggest ways to train and encourage such men

SCRIPTURE READING

For even the Son of Man came not to be served but to serve, and to give his life as a ransom for many.

—Mark 10:45

And what you have heard from me in the presence of many witnesses entrust to faithful men who will be able to teach others also.

—2 Timothy 2:2

LECTURE OUTLINE

A. A healthy church must be concerned for the spread of the gospel both geographically and generationally.
   1. Pastors and elders need to think about the faith generationally.
      a. Paul's exhortation to Timothy to entrust the gospel to others contains four spiritual generations (2 Tim. 2:2).

      b. Pastors and elder need to entrust the faith to men who will entrust it to others, praying for those they have raised up and sent for God's glory.

      c. Pastors have a responsibility after identifying men with the biblical qualifications to encourage them to grow.

B. There are nine marks helpful to identifying, growing, and training elders.

   1. Pastors and elders must find men who meet the biblical qualifications.

      a. The biblical qualifications for an elder can be found in 1 Timothy 3 and Titus 1.

      b. Identifying and discerning the qualifications in men and encouraging their growth in Christ is not a form of favoritism.

      c. It is important that men have a desire for the office (1 Tim. 3:1).

   2. Pastors and elders must look for the men God is raising up around them.

      a. The men who are evangelizing and helping others grow will be evident if pastors and elders look for them.

      b. God is ultimately at work in these men and in the church, and since God is doing the work, the church of Christ will be victorious.

      c. Pastors and elders must interact with the congregation by creating events so that qualified men can surface.

      d. Pastors should regularly pray through their membership directory in order to bring candidates to mind.

   3. Pastors and elders must trust and be charitable.

      a. Pastors and elders are sometimes too cautious in the opportunities they give men within the church.

      b. Pastors and elders should be willing to trust men by giving them opportunities to see what they do with them.

      c. Pastors and elders can take risks on qualified men and observe how their teaching and leadership abilities develop.

      d. God is ultimately at work in handing down the faith; the Great Commission is not only geographical, it's chronological.

   4. Pastors and elders need to be willing to invest personal time.

      a. Jesus demonstrates this in the way He gathered His disciples and lived among them, pouring His life into them before He sent them.

      b. Just as Paul pointed to Himself as an example, pastors and elders are examples of Christ to the church (1 Cor. 11:1; Phil. 3:17; Heb. 13:7).

      c. Pastors and elders need to be creative in finding ways to spend time with a small group of men they are eager to train.

   5. Pastors and elders need to delegate responsibility to others.

      a. Pastors and elders have a responsibility to cultivate the respect of the congregation for younger leaders.

      b. Pastors and elders should give men opportunities to teach and keep the legacy of their own ministries in mind for the next generation.

   6. Pastors and elders need to be able to give and receive feedback.

      a. Pastors and elders must be willing to receive feedback so as not to create prideful, self-defensive ministry.

      b. Pastors and elders should be models for giving godly criticism because they know how important truthful friends are.
      c. Paul is an example of how to acknowledge God's work by giving godly encouragement to the Corinthians (1 Cor. 1:1–9).
7. Pastors and elders need a right understanding of authority.
      a. Pastors and elders must rule justly (2 Sam. 23:1–4).
      b. Pastors and elders must find men who understand that ruling justly is a blessing to others.
8. Pastors and elders must find men who have clarity and an ability to teach, men who have an ability to explain doctrine and answer difficult questions.
9. Pastors and elders must encourage humility.
      a. Pastors and elders set themselves as an example in training up younger men by not being threatened by their ability to lead.
      b. Pastors and elders must use their God-given gifts to humbly assess and create space for young men to grow in their God-given gifts.

STUDY QUESTIONS

1. James' warning against favoritism should extend the specialized training of elders to every man in a congregation.
      a. True
      b. False

2. Paul's exhortation to Timothy to hand down the faith contains _____ spiritual generations.
      a. Two
      b. Three
      c. Four
      d. Five

3. People often forget that the Great Commission is _____.
      a. Geographical
      b. Chronological
      c. Theological
      d. Rhetorical

4. Trust and opportunities should only be given to a qualified man after he goes through a thorough period of testing.
      a. True
      b. False

5. _____ is an essential defense against a prideful, self-defensive ministry.
      a. Trust
      b. Feedback

c. Delegation
d. Encouragement

6. Paul's acknowledgment of God's work at the beginning of 1 Corinthians shows the importance of _____.
    a. Trust
    b. Authority
    c. Feedback
    d. Encouragement

DISCUSSION QUESTIONS

1. Dr. Dever suggests ways for pastors to identify men for leadership in the church. What are some of the ways you have identified the spiritual authorities in your own life?

2. Why does Dr. Dever look for natural gifts of leadership in addition to the biblical qualifications of an elder? Do you think everyone should strive to develop such characteristics?

3. Consider the qualifications of an elder in 1 Timothy 3 and Titus 1. Do you think it is hopeless for someone who does not currently meet the qualifications to strive after them?

4. How important is a right understanding of authority for the church? Especially consider recent cultural developments that are resistant to authority.

15

Reasons to Join a Church

INTRODUCTION

If you want to be a healthy Christian, you need to be a part of a healthy church. In this lesson, Dr. Dever gives reasons to join a local church—a practice that is obligatory for the Christian and has served as the pattern for Christians since the first century.

LESSON OBJECTIVES

1. To emphasize the importance of joining a church
2. To underscore the benefits of joining a church

SCRIPTURE READING

And they devoted themselves to the apostles' teaching and the fellowship, to the breaking of bread and the prayers.

—Acts 2:42

LECTURE OUTLINE

A. Join a church as a commitment to holy love.
   1. Joining a church is the only way to obey the biblical commands to love one another (John 13:35; 1 John 4:20).
   2. Jesus Christ is the model of Christian love, so we seek to love one another in the same way that He loved us, which means we have sincere love for sinners.
   3. Being a member of a local church is a commitment to encourage one another to love and good works (Heb. 10:23–25).

B. Join a church as a powerful witness.
   1. The church is Jesus' evangelism program.
      a. The world knows that we are Christ's disciples by our love for one another (John 13:35).
      b. The gospel is illustrated by our love for one another, especially as we forgive one another.
   2. The Christian concept of love is entirely foreign to the world.

C. Join a church for an assurance of holy love.
   1. The church has an obligation to holy love through the sacraments to affirm or deny its agreement with an individual's profession.
   2. First Corinthians 5 is a passage that shows a church's obligation to assure an individual that his profession is in accordance with true Christian faith.
   3. Church membership functions to assure us that we are not self-deceived, that we know God's love and truly love Him in return (2 Cor. 13:15).

D. Join a church to teach about the nature of true love.
   1. The local church is the context in which we are obedient and display our love for our brothers, which assures us that we are Christians (1 John 3:11–19).
   2. Christians are called to love others even when it is inconvenient, and the only way to avoid loving selectively is by joining a local church.
   3. The world knows how to love people who are considered worthy of love, but it does not know the type of divine love displayed in a church.

E. Join a church to learn about obedience to holy love.
   1. Church membership displays a committed love to obey particular leaders as commanded by the Bible (Heb. 13:17).
   2. Church membership displays an understanding that authority and love can exist together, that abuses of power do not delegitimize all authority.
   3. Throughout creation, authority is intended to be an expression of God's own character, so that authority well exercised blesses others.

F. Join a church to display the glory of love.
   1. Christ created the church as an expression of His own nature and character, which is why the actions of the church reflect on Him and His glory.
      a. Christ takes an attack upon the church as an attack upon Himself (Acts 9:4).
      b. God is praised and glorified by our actions (1 Peter 2:12).
   2. Church membership is our duty as Christian's, as beneficial to ourselves, the church, and also the world that needs to see God's love on display.

STUDY QUESTIONS

1. Mindfulness of the approaching day of judgment and encouraging others as part of a local church are related.
    a. True
    b. False

2. According to Dr. Dever, joining a local church is a means to obey the imperative to _____.
    a. Love
    b. Grow
    c. Trust
    d. Serve

3. Joining a local church enables you to love when it is _____.
    a. Expected
    b. Desirable
    c. Inconvenient
    d. Reciprocated

4. An abuse of authority does not delegitimize authority.
    a. True
    b. False

5. Joining the local church and your _____ are closely related.
    a. Profession
    b. Obedience
    c. Assurance
    d. All of the above

6. Christ's marked question to _____ shows how closely He identifies with the church.
    a. John
    b. Stephen
    c. Saul
    d. Peter

DISCUSSION QUESTIONS

1. What are some experiences you have had as a Christian that are encouragements for others to join a local church?

2. What are ways you can encourage non-members in your church to commit to membership? How would you explain the personal and familial benefits of church membership to them?

3. What would you say to a professing Christian who voices hesitations about joining a church?

4. How does Christ identify with the church? How does His identification with the church provide reasons for joining a church?

ANSWER KEY FOR STUDY QUESTIONS

Lesson 1
1. A
2. C
3. B
4. B
5. A
6. D

Lesson 2
1. A
2. D
3. A
4. B
5. B
6. C

Lesson 3
1. B
2. D
3. D
4. B
5. A
6. D

Lesson 4
1. B
2. B
3. D
4. B
5. C
6. D

Lesson 5
1. B
2. A
3. C
4. B
5. D
6. C

Lesson 6
1. B
2. D
3. B
4. B
5. A
6. C

Lesson 7
1. B
2. B
3. D
4. A
5. B
6. A

Lesson 8
1. B
2. B
3. D
4. B
5. C
6. D

Lesson 9
1. B
2. A
3. A
4. A
5. D
6. D

Lesson 10
1. B
2. C
3. B
4. B
5. C
6. D

Lesson 11
1. B
2. B
3. C
4. B
5. B
6. A

Lesson 12
1. B
2. D
3. B
4. B
5. D
6. D

Lesson 13
1. A
2. C
3. D
4. A
5. D
6. D

Lesson 14
1. B
2. C
3. B
4. B
5. B
6. D

Lesson 15
1. A
2. A
3. C
4. A
5. D
6. C